nat[a]

TO Alex,
Thank you for supporting me! It was so
great to meet you today :)

north

star

heart

Natasha Silm

TSPA THE SELF PUBLISHING AGENCY, INC.

Natasha Silva

North Star Heart

TSPA The Self Publishing Agency, Inc.

Acknowledgement is gratefully given to Event magazine for which the following poems originally appeared: "From the Girl Who Loves the Forest More Than Herself" & "Uncertain Feelings for These Unknown Places."

Cover & Book Illustrations | Q Silva
Book Design | Kristy Twellmann Hill

Editor | Alison Whyte

Publishing Support | TSPA The Self Publishing Agency, Inc.

acknowledgements

I'd like to thank everyone who has had a part in making this book a reality:

my family and friends for always being willing readers and offering their never-ending support,

my professors and fellow cohort students from UBC for their feedback on early drafts of these poems,

and my entire team at TSPA for helping me launch *North Star Heart* into the world.

preface

The North Star is a symbol of direction, of finding one's way, and is most often referred to in a navigational sense. But what happens when we are not physically lost yet still haven't found our way home? I believe we all have our own North Stars. They are not in the sky but instead beat internally within us: our North Star Hearts. They are there to guide us to where we're meant to be whether that's a physical destination, a spiritual connection, a shift in our mentalities, or an important relationship not yet forged. The needs of these North Star Hearts are intense, confusing, and visceral, but when heeded can lead to the most rewarding journeys of self-discovery.

Over the last few years, my North Star Heart has been steadily pointing me toward northern places—small, close-knit communities, bigger mountains, and rural landscapes. I know I am embarking on a North Star Heart journey when I get an overwhelming, total-body feeling of belonging. This can be to a place or an idea and can even come through interactions. I know I've found my way to that journey's destination when that same feeling of belonging returns as I walk the streets or trails it's taken me to or have conversations with the people it's introduced me to. My North Star Heart beats deep within me; it's where my biggest emotions live and has been the cause of some of my most significant self-realizations. I'm simultaneously ruled by it and in awe of the places it's taken me and the things it's shown me about myself.

Perhaps the journey I'm describing is a familiar one. Or maybe it sounds daunting because there are still obstacles preventing that exploration for you. Your North Star Heart journey may take you to the tops of mountains, the shores of lakes, or the streets of a country you never thought you'd visit. It will reveal not only the nature of the outside world but also the nature that guides who you are. Feeling lost can be a catalyst for these journeys that ultimately lead us to the home we have been seeking all along.

I

when i close my eyes, this is what i dream about

It's November. The days favour dark, the sky coats
itself in the same shade of grey from morning to night.
The rain now relentless against my windshield like pebbles
wailing from the sky and exploding across the glass. Relentless
against my back, a constant shove to move faster, think harder,
be prepared. Relentless against my face, drops slip
down like tears. I just want to get in my car and drive.

Drive until the rain turns to snow and every tree wears
a white cap. Drive and worry around every turn
because I don't have four-wheel drive.
Drive until the snow falls thick and suspended
by its own weight. I'll pull over and let the cotton flakes
coat my eyelashes until they're heavy. Let my hair cool
and lighten until I am all flake and gravity no longer exists.

I want to find a small Christmas town. One where the residents
bake cookies for each other. One where the carolers come out
when the weather hits the right temperature. One where
the people welcome seeing another person with a smile
and a gesture instead of pulling out a phone or turning to face
the other way while still moving forward. One where almost everyone
owns a practical plaid with insulation for negative weather.

I want to wake up by natural light in a bed piled with blankets
to a view of the mountains. Mountains that stretch their jagged
necks high into the clouds while their bases sit stout
on the outer edges of town. Mountains with forests, needled
trees so green I feel my brain start spitting lines from the colour alone.
Mountains with ice-capped peaks only visible
when the sun shines full. Mountains with peaks begging to be explored.
Begging to not be alone in their isolation.

I want to be in a coffee shop with books and people who carry
wonderment like a stone in their pocket and a need to explore
as a compass in their core. My fingers will run
across my keyboard with fever. My ideas flashing so fast
it feels like losing hours switching time zones and if my hands stop
those ideas will be miles away. And no matter how fast
I run I will never catch up to them.

I want to take long walks down salted streets until my legs feel numb
but not from the cold. Hands in parka pockets, fingers etch patterns
in the fabric and I'll think about what it would be like to belong
to a town that can make any stray feel home.

u n s u s t a i n e d

The Cloud spites me,
wind tosses sand with no water,
paper-cuts my hope.
I am the last weather worshipper;
he won't watch as my faith bleeds out.

The Pacific yells at the Cloud.
He responds: strikes trees 'til they fall,
their bodies lie unprotected.
The Pacific tips boats
without checking their capacity,
(none of them were empty)
neither apologizes.

The Cloud bellows
and the wind cuts my cheeks,
splinters my skin like it's made of the driftwood
that used to keep me company.

The Cloud ignores the Honourable Mother Nature,
thunders his disagreement with lightning blows,
responds to legal channels with the promise of more burnt trees.
Their ashes have already overtaken the airways.

The Pacific is reminded of this attack daily.
Branches aflame wave a goodbye.
The wind carries those last words,
ignites the grass with them;
the fire tumbles in every direction.

The Pacific tries to save them;
ten-foot waves eradicate roots,
carry the fire to a salted tomb.
I am the only witness
and I am invalidated by Mother Nature's gavel.

I imagine walking in,
let the Pacific wrap her arms around me
until I'm as blue as my insides.

amar você seria um erro

There's a taste my mouth has been missing.
A smoky, between midnight and three am,
highway, beef jerky, and spearmint gum mixture.
A gasoline spill while a forest fire grows kind of taste.

I've never tasted gasoline
accented by the ashes of trees,
and I've never kissed you.
But I'm sure you kiss her.
Maybe you like that mix
of bubblegum and peach cooler.
Maybe it's easier for you to taste her.

I'm a double shot of espresso
and a single of paint-thinner tequila.
I won't give you a chase.
I'm bitter followed by a burn.

You dream of VIP lounges
and peach cooler girl on your arm.
I wouldn't adorn your limbs.
You'd have to grow thorns,
prick me into place.

But rumours of our kiss
would inspire the most original album
of our generation.
Hit singles, still favourited thirty years later,
after we're divorced,
and our wayward sons and daughters
are finding trails to call home.

Amar você seria um erro,
amar você seria um erro,
amar você seria um erro.

If we kissed, it'd be a mistake.
But I wouldn't mind.

There's poetry in being hurt.

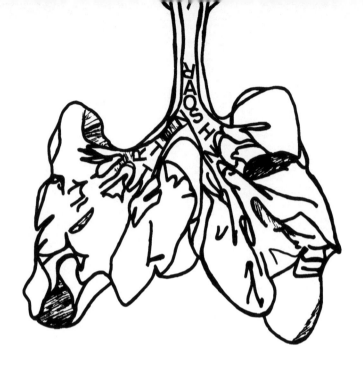

impaired

Your name's a plosive; the letters choke my lungs, release
their grip after the last syllable, exhale
as loud as the espresso machines.
They and the counter fill the space between us;
fill the gaps in the words we didn't say.

The effects of sleep deprivation:
an increased risk of forgetting "I love you"s
you never really felt that way
(but that's okay).

h e a v y

My thoughts have been twisting
like fog weaves through corn rows.
My neurons press then scatter
as decisions ebb and settle.

It's October, all I see are pine needles.
I'm waiting for them to hurricane around me:
draw blood until my skin's grated finer
than the rotten leaves that blanket the street.
I'm waiting for my body to revert until it's hollow.

Happiness is heavy;
I'm worried my heart will reject it
like a surrogate skin graft.

lover's cpr

I (Summer)

She straddles you
in your father's Mustang: dark blue
like the sky after a fiery sunset.
Both of you rest,
inhale, exhale, into each other,
locked in a lover's CPR.
Both of you tremble.
It's the middle of August,
but together it's twenty below zero.

II (Autumn)

You get onto the bus;
she slips her heart into your backpack
like a book you'd forgotten.
But the Pacific is too big a divide,
and months later
you look at the ocean
like it's stolen her from you.
Right now, you're still blinded
by ocean brine
but the sea salt hurts her eyes too.

where do you go when your heart doesn't know its way?

I

Gales gust unseen from moody skies,
the edge of the breakwater beckons me

closer

close enough
to feel salt sting from whiplash winds
and no longer feel numb
skin under soaked shirts,

start to fill my gaping chest cavity
as the ocean tries to make me whole.

II

Branches envelope and call
me *home*
when my heart no longer has one.
Organ floats on needles,
growing, it balloons
until it meets the sky: untethered

I remain.

My husk rests on the forest floor,
hollow but feeling remnants
of what I once marked happiness.

III

Climbing to stony crags forces
my heart to work.
Shows tough love,

you must beat to make it

to the peak.
My body drifts along mountain views
leaving my brain and heart to argue
where they'll be safe
and how to protect
the body that hauls them.

from the girl who loves the forest more than herself

It's the forest I tell my graveyard secrets to.
The trees gather the words
in the folds of their branches,
pass them from cedar to Douglas fir to pine.

The mountain peaks draw energy
from the darkest parts of me,
transform marred memories to ones of bliss
and uplift me to cumulus cloud status.
The vistas manipulate heartbeats.
They speed up so fast I can fly
almost as high as the whiskey jacks on Cypress.

The sun sets over the valley,
the blue of the Fraser, iridescent
against the dying light.
The breeze blows my secrets through the evergreens
and that burning sky tattoos the tree line to my retinas.
(These secrets won't die with me.)

revelaciones de bachata

Requinto starts soft, grows
mesmerizing, crafts each step
as I glide sultry toward you
cut through partners,
Dominican step past a closing bar
eye contact: blue
but with a foreign softness

no break as we *slide*
hold until the '2'
pressure building with the bass guitar
releases on '4' when the *segunda*
reminds us there is a rhythm

tempo increases, we join
hands, move in time
hips circle with each step
midnight on the dance floor,
but our bodies move like it's 2am
and we're already under the sheets

bongo crescendos as you lead
us into the *cuddle*
four counts forward, four counts backward,
return to *basic step* I close
the gap, let our bodies speak
the words we've held since last January.

b o r e a l   r e u n i o n

Arctic pressures blow
our names as we sleep,
one syllable
         at
            a
                time.

Fifty-below winds unearth ruptured promises,
scatter words we didn't mean across the tundra,
leave us with a chill
            blankets
                    won't
                        cure.

North Star Hearts bind us with borealis lights,
green and purple weave through the somber sky,
illuminate the path back home
                to
                    each
                        other.

II

whiskey words

My pen slurs the words
I don't speak.
Slanted black calligraphy:
the translator for whirlpool minds.
This time frustration sails
through the barrel.

This ink has seen individuals
intoxicated by more
than the alcohol.
It knows I'm not drunk
from the scotch.

The original intoxication
is not being plastered.
It's having all the words
and trying to speak them.
They don't make sense:
crack capillaries to create lines,
break bones for stanzas.

A poet knows the body
is not on a schedule.
This is why wine
can be for Wednesday mornings
and words are not born on time.

Those empty bottles lining the counter
are full of escaping phrases,
every lost one is mourned.
That girl writing at the bar is not drunk.
Her severed tongue is trying to speak.

uncertain feelings for
these unknown places

He drowns each cigarette drag with coffee.
We don't share thoughts on this unfamiliar road.
Smoky exhale, I wonder what makes him happy
as I keep my undetermined feelings stowed.

We don't share thoughts on this unfamiliar road.
I spend half an hour concentrating on passing cars,
as I keep my undetermined feelings stowed.
I tell him I'm fond of scars.

I spend half an hour concentrating on passing cars,
don't confess I'm thinking about being with him.
I tell him I'm fond of scars.
Ask him, what's the worst thing he's done on a whim?

I don't confess I'm thinking about being with him.
The sun's going down. Sleep's an inevitable issue.
I ask him, what's the worst thing he's done on a whim?
Write a song about the combination of our tissues.

Sun's going down, sleep's an inevitable issue,
we can afford a hotel. But, we crash on reclined seats.
Write a song about the combination of our tissues,
ask him to leave on the heat.

We can afford a hotel, but we crash on reclined seats.
Another smoky exhale. I still wonder what makes him happy.
Ask him to leave on the heat,
he drowns each cigarette drag with coffee.

remainders

I hope we live like tattoos:
an artistic open wound.
A reminder that permanent art
requires pain and maybe
that's why reaching the sunrise
hurts so much without you.

Talking to you was the best poem
I ever wrote and lately,
I've had this writer's block
like I stuck my tongue in honey
and it cemented when you left.

snowflake memories

The snow makes me miss you
more than usual.
You've been stuck on my mind
since the first flake landed
upon my outstretched hands.

international identity
ruminations

I

It's the Portuguese in me rolling on Oura beach,
coating myself in a layer of fine sand like a powdered donut.
I close my eyes to wake up with the Atlantic reaching out.
Dive into the cold relief and resurface
in the forty-degree heat, bask like um lagarto ao sol.
Walk home sun drunk and salty with a tin of takeout polvo.

II

I lounge at the top of Tâmpa Mountain,
finally grasping my Canadian self:
the part of me that longs for tired, dusty legs
and hours of hiking through tree stands
trying to name each high elevation species.
The peace of canvas walls, sleeping bag heat preservation,
and desire to explore the surrounding forest for weeks.

III

The pieces of my identity float,
caught in a thunderstorm
where the Sava and Danube meet:
the Canadian in me craves dense snowfall and negative weather,
watches the sky for purple clouds pregnant with flakes to fall
and plunges into untouched banks with my dogs close behind.
I embrace the Belgrade rain with arms spread,
let it pelt realization until my jacket is a second skin
and I almost miss Vancouver's rainy afternoons.

IV

Identity fragments start connecting in a car
full of creatives on an unfinished road to Tara Canyon:
the Portuguese in me yearns to put my hands in the dirt.
Pluck berries from bushes, squish and ferment into wine
swirling my glass three months later.
In Canada, chicken chatter is my morning ritual;
Quinta do Rio farming blood pumps steadily
in me a generation after immigration.

rainy week in the rockies

Into the forest I go to lose my mind and find my soul.
—attributed to John Muir, on a bathroom wall in Jasper, AB

I find it in the quiet
wind rustles, branches fan:
show their summer greens.
Peaks hide under rain mist
and I am out of body
hovering over a lake bluer
than any eyes I've ever loved.

It's there,
where I am unprotected
and must trust in the land I've traversed
that it will let me see tomorrow.

It's there.
I find the hum within myself
it tells me who I am,
where to find my feet when I am locked
in constant free fall. Where I need to go
to hear that hum resonate until my chest
still rumbles at the memory.

In these lands, I am mindless.
I am bodiless.
It's where I must be to discover
every part that makes me.

backroads

He drives and sings softly
to a tune about a small-town boy.
Stubble's grown in enough to prick my cheeks
but not a full beard yet.

The trees have changed
postcard perfect in my vision.
Forested hills are deep green with small stands
of yellow breaking through like pocketed sunshine.

We animal spot as we drive.
Mule deer are everywhere:
four to the left,
two in the back field,
three grazing to the right.
Doe eyes concentrate on the blades they chew.
One black bear, you saw (I didn't)
ran uphill into the trees.

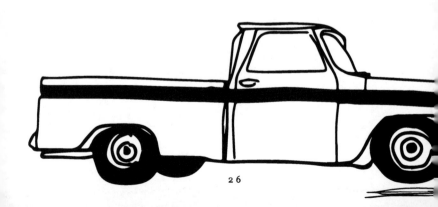

Wheels wind up the mountainside,
stumble over bumps,
we drive to the right, left, both lanes.
Rain rumbles against the windshield,
fog hugs the trees tight,
green leaves try to remain
while yellow and orange overtake.
The others have already lost their leaves;
they will face winter bare and bony.

Truck grumbles over the cattle guard
honks echo lightly
the cows decided to block
both lanes of non-existent traffic.
The babies don't know what to do:
run in front of the truck before veering
back to the bushes where their family waits.

One hand on the wheel,
you grasp my hand in yours.
365 days of you and I
keeps us smiling every mile
along this coloured country backroad.

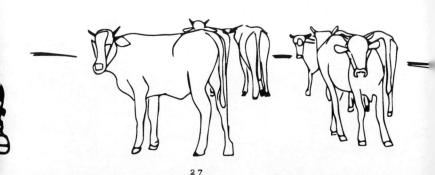

springtime awakening

Gravel crunches under my boots,
cedar scents linger along the trails
I used to call home.
The ghost of 18-year-old me rushes
without noticing the quiver
of a fluffy tail but now I lock
eyes until the squirrel
scampers into the canopy.

Daffodils begin to surface,
the ground's softer
where their heads emerge:
bulbous, waiting to unfurl.
Frosted patches fade with warmth
from the spring sun,
like the flowers I uplift
myself to meet its gaze.

I pause at the river's edge,
hold my breath so I don't alert
a still-fat-from-winter beaver
emerging from its dam.
Watch it paddle with newly collected
twigs in its overstuffed mouth,
rays beaming off its water-slicked fur.
It lets the branches go and we both
stop for a clean breath of air.

100 mile welcome

Tongue thick with sauv blanc
I exit our log cabin and light the end
of my Upmann, quick draws
until flame flows, wrap crackles,
and tobacco smoke engulfs
the last trace of wine, hold
before I release a full plume
into the midnight Cariboo air.

My balance is off, a realization
as my knees buckle stepping off the deck.
My brain somersaults with each stumbled stride
until I reach the worn dirt pathway
leading out the ranch gates.
Loon calls sound from the lake,
eerie like they're far away
but I can still see the water's gleam.

My cigar warms the fingers of my right hand,
I draw deep and stop to look skyward.
The Big Dipper waves to me blanketed
by thousands of stars embedded in the Milky Way.
I turn in small circles and the stars swirl;
a blend of light shines down like the sky
is saying, "you can belong here."

III

the bulkley sentinels

I wake to my name ringing
over the valley and wish
I could answer the giants
who summon me:

embark on my pilgrimage
to leave the snow-coated asphalt,
traverse into silver-tipped evergreens,
get blinded by fog at the sub peak,
yell the sentinels' names
when my lungs are at capacity
and air is fleeting.
Whisper, thank you
when their winds restore it.

Legs quake like a 5.5
magnitude tectonic shift
and I drop to my knees
in worship at the summit.
Exude gratitude from each shining pore,
as I gaze down at the town
I thought only existed in dreams.

observations on main

Hudson Bay Mountain stands formidable
on the outskirts of town.
Wears a white fluffed coat,
endures rough winds and cutting
snow with a straight back.

Logs crackle in the chalet fire,
grey stones stained charcoal.
My face basks in my laptop's glow,
Word's open, paragraphs flow.
Orange pekoe steam winds and curls
like the spine of a bachata dancer.
The brown paper cup warms my palms.

Snowplow piles stack street sides,
shuffle-step tracks mark sidewalk paths.
Journal pages lay coated with scrawl;
my pen hurries but my thoughts fog.
My fingertips drum along the spruce counter
as little white flakes drift from purple skies
to land upon twinkle lights lined down Main.

to nechako, 'cause i can't stop thinking about you

I'm aching to see your backroads,
how mountains curve into roadways,
and open fields lay coated in winter snow.
I want to count how many leaf hues
litter the same fields in autumn.

I want to discover if your boreal arteries
make me plunge into love as fast
as the Douglas firs and lodgepole pines weaving
through the Cariboo Chilcotin backcountry did.

I want to come back to see grizzlies
roam mountainsides and moose
wander through backyards.
Explore woods and meadows on horseback,
feeling every up and down connection
with the earth through galloping hooves.

I'll plant roots and learn to predict
spring by the names of deciduous
trees regaining their leaves
and resident deer returning with fawns.
Spell out my story with each fleck
of dirt off my boots until we've spent
years learning about each other.

tennessee date night

Banjo twangs jumpstart me into black leather
boots-pointed toes-dancing shoes.
Fireball's tucked against my shin,
sloshes with every two-step spin.
Felt hat–clad cowboy with a whiskey flask
peeking above a Wrangler waistband
offers a hand and we start:

little step, bigger step,
he guides me in a circle
pulls close when the fiddle squeals
pushes far when the harmonica flutters
reels me back: quick spin, big dip and repeat.

The crowd shifts, we rush
to find our own spaces in the last row
of this country line dance floor.
Refresh ourselves with the Fireball
in my boot, alternate with his whiskey,
passing bottles on each rotation.
My vision blurs, the fiddle sings,
plaid arms link out the barn doors,
and the banjo echoes down the dirt road home.

will it be?

10 years from now,
I wonder if it will be you
two-stepping with me
from the kitchen to the living room,
wearing red plaids still damp
from the fresh flakes falling.

We'll switch to bachata as the song changes
sing along in shitty Spanish accents
let smiles stretch until we collapse
into each other on the couch
giggling, like we did when we were 20.

pinecone blueprints

We laid in a forested oval,
tucked in by blades of grass,
housed by ten-foot pines.
I told you it was where I wanted
us to spend our forever.

We loved the way ice cubes melt:
individuals returning to the same water.
We had a sense of family,
like salmon traversing back
to their birthplace to lay their eggs.
We always came back to each other,
no matter how far away we had drifted
or how long it took to traverse back.

You made pinecone blueprints,
mapped out the same number
of bedrooms nestled in my head.
Told me you knew
'cause our DNA's already intertwined.
We didn't need a two-toned stick
to tell us the result was positive.

I wondered if our daughter
would find our meadow
like a pre-programmed map location,
directed by steady feet and a stable mind.
Would she find her birthplace the same way salmon do?

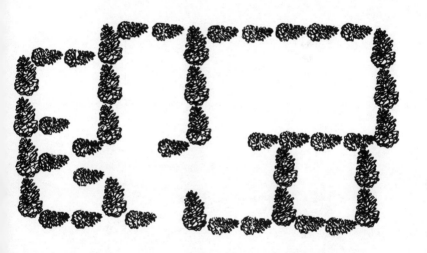

39

postcard christmases

I

We build our home
at 54.7824° N, 127.1686° W.
Dress our house with glass
windows facing the mountains
and overlooking the barn and pastures
soon to be occupied
like the bedrooms inside.

II

The steam from our mugs creates
condensation on frosted windows
as we watch trees bend
with the weight of snow
and our horses clad in plaid blankets
kick fluffy drifts with each prance.

I bundle our kids until they waddle
like overdressed penguins.
Tumbling in snow up to their tummies
they belly slide from the front door.

We cuddle them between us
and tour the back forty in the sleigh you crafted
when we discovered our first was on the way.
Ask if they've spotted Rudolph hiding in the boreal;
they aren't old enough to know him as a caribou yet.

III

We hunt for a live tree every year,
examine the needles
for the direction they face
and if the green is silvered or yellowed.
Argue over balsam, Douglas, or Fraser.

Teach our kids how to dig around the tree
and contain it with a burlap root ball
so we can plant it in the new year:
create a grove of Christmas trees past.

plaid winter

Steam swirls from the surface
of my strawberry mulled wine.
Cinnamon and star anise slide down,
warm me from the inside.

Snow falls to coat my collie's fur
she kicks snowballs,
snatches mouthfuls, and barks
when I make eye contact.

I crouch to embrace her
tongue warms my cheek,
she prances for praise
dusting herself with disturbed snow.
I pour a sip of mulled wine,
she pounces on the pink frozen treat.

I transfer the remaining contents
to a travel mug, lock the lid, and run.
Legs slog through the depth,
leaving a human paved trail behind.

She leads the way until I am thigh
deep in the back forty.
I fall backwards with my mug
to my red-checked chest
and let her dig me out.

thanksgiving tradition

Snow trails loftily, caresses my face,
and sinks into the synthetic sleeves
of my favourite camo jacket.
We've maintained our position
in the blind for five hours.
Both lying prone, only our boots touch,
scanning opposite directions for the target.

The stock of my Remington sits snug,
shoulder acutely aware of its power,
I lower it for a moment.
You nudge my weathered ceramic mug
over the thin tarp we lay upon,
I sip on lukewarm coffee,
feel the cup shake in my tired grip.

Alert to a crack and the sight of long tines
barely visible through the branches.
Sweeping antlers, grace in every step,
he prances into the clearing, and we readjust our scopes.
One tap against my boot: you have the shot
and I ready myself for a secondary.

I listen to your exhale
and the sound of the bullet
releasing from the bore riots
through the hemlock cover.
We grasp gloved hands,
wait for the bull elk to exert his last breath,
grateful for the harvest we are about to receive.

dirt road culture

This is where the tractor will chew and spit dirt,
churning fields where my children will learn
to shoot: position stocks into shoulders
and lay hesitant fingertips over trigger guards.

This is where they'll embrace
the farmhood in their blood:
corral the goats back when they escape,
plant carefully cultivated seedlings,
and yell at the chickens when they fly
into their barely blooming garden beds.

This is where they will be baptised.
First by holy water,
second by aged aguardente.
Instructed in our languages
and those the trees speak
as seasons change, plants shrivel,
and animals migrate away.

This is where they'll discover their origins.
Revealed by visiting family
sharing secret stories loosened
by a half empty port bottle,
the smell of frango on the rotisserie,
and the taste of home in the July air.

author bio

Natasha Silva is a dual citizen of Canada and Portugal; she is a graduate of the University of British Columbia's School of Creative Writing and has been previously published by Event magazine and Polar Expressions Publishing. She is driven and often inspired by the natural world around her, particularly rugged mountain ranges, old-growth forests, and secluded beaches. When not writing, she can be found walking her dogs, tending to her farm animals, sitting atop a mountain, or in an airport awaiting her next adventure.

Made in the USA
Columbia, SC
26 October 2021